St Rita Convent

D1094342

MONKS OF MT. TABOR

Shepherds in the Mist

Shepherds in the Mist

E. BOYD BARRETT

THE DECLAN X. McMULLEN COMPANY, INC.
NEW YORK

NIHIL OBSTAT
   Amancio Rodriguez, S. T. D.
      Censor librorum

IMPRIMATUR
   ✠ A. J. Willinger, C. SS. R.
      Monterey-Fresno Ordinary

Fresno, California
July 1, 1949

Copyright 1949
THE DECLAN X. McMULLEN COMPANY, INC.
Printed in the U. S. A.

CONTENTS

PREFACE

In december, 1948, i wrote an article in *America* entitled "Prayer for Stray Shepherds." It was, as its title indicates, an appeal for spiritual help for priests in trouble, priests who had gone astray. To my title the editor of *America* added as subtitle, "They Are Still Ours." His was a touching, a beautiful suggestion, and it is the slogan-thought underlying this book.

The article was reprinted in many Catholic papers, in many countries and languages, and it finally appeared in the Vatican City journal,

Ecclesia. It seemed plain that the Catholic world wanted to understand better the sad fortune of their priests in trouble, in order to help them more.

The letters that came to me as a result of my article in *America* were a revelation. I had not dreamed that there was, or could be, so much sympathy or love in the hearts of the Catholic people for their missing shepherds, lost in the wilderness. When I was out there myself, an excommunicated priest, bitter and resentful, I never realized that thousands, most of them complete strangers, were praying and doing penance for me.

Letters that brought tears to my eyes came to me from nuns and layfolk, telling how they had fought on through the years for my return to Christ. In this little book I want to tell *all* "Stray Shepherds" that for each of them the same kind of heroic fight is being waged.

The purpose of my writing this development of my *America* article is very simple. I know now that *you,* fellow Catholics, have charity in your hearts for priests in trouble. I know that you pray for them. But you will want to know, among other things, if there is any way in which you can help them, over and above praying for them. And now you will want to be encouraged to pray even more than you are praying and to sacrifice yourselves even more than you are doing for their sakes.

But, besides thinking of you, fellow Catholics of good standing, I am also thinking of our Shepherds in the mist. Some of them will read this book. There are things I want to tell *them*. Above all, I want to disabuse them of their fear that you have feelings of dislike and resentment against them. I want to tell them that the one burning thought in your minds is how to induce them to come home. I want to reassure them of the fact that it is not hard to come home—to reassure them that, however rugged his exterior may seem, Peter is kind and gentle with the kindliness and gentleness of Christ.

When a son runs away from home, his mother's one thought is how to get him back again. She worries over his loneliness and sufferings. It is of the dangers that he is in that she thinks, and of the hardships he is undergoing—not of the faults he has committed. She does not remember the wrong her son has done her by running away; she but dreams of the joy it will be for her when he returns.

Our Stray Shepherds see their home from afar. It is never out of sight, never quite forgotten. They see the door open, the lights burning, and familiar figures moving about. They cannot *feel* its warmth till they recross the threshold—then they will know again what Christ's love is!

I will try to write simply and honestly, asking Mary to guide my hand. I will try to be a faithful messenger, my brother Stray Shepherd, as I carry to you the Bethany message of long ago: "The Master is here and calleth for *you!*"

E. Boyd Barrett

I

LAST CHANCE

THERE ARE NUNS AND LAYFOLK WHO CON-
secrate their lives to the wonderful mystical
work of prayer and sacrifice for priests. They
realize with marvellous clarity that the Good
Shepherd *needs* other good shepherds. They
realize that His work succeeds in direct propor-
tion to the virtue and efficiency of His shepherds. By their heroic prayers and penances
they win great graces for priests; and priests,
more than any others, need great graces, for
they live close to the edge of peril.

1

Because priests know at close quarters the meaning of danger, since they are the front line of the Church's defenses, they have more than any others real and deep sympathy with their brother priests who have failed. They are always ready to help them—always ready to say a good word about them. And they keep them in mind affectionately. It is some good priest, too, who has the last word with our Stray Shepherd—some good priest who has been empowered to offer him a *last chance*.

For the nuns and layfolk who pray for priests, not only for the faithful ones but for *all* priests, it may be helpful to paint the scene of a Stray Shepherd's last chance. Too often—every week, perhaps—somewhere or other—in some form or other—this scene repeats itself. It is the dread moment against which prayers should be stored up. It is a moment of supreme importance when a word—nay, even a handshake, may turn the scales for good. It is a moment that needs to be understood by those in whose eyes all priests are Christ's.

There is always a last chance. It is offered in one form or another. Christ does not part with His own easily. I think that often, very often, the offer is not made in vain. The priest in trouble, the priest on the point of flight, is

2

saved at the last moment. Some heartfelt prayer, some heroic sacrifice on the part of a humble sister who has devoted her life to the welfare of God's shepherds, wins grace and light. Instead of turning his back on Christ and hurrying into the dark night, the priest presses his crucifix to his breast.

The scene of the last chance is the scene of a struggle between good and evil, wisdom and folly, humility and pride. It is the scene of a momentous struggle. God only knows how much depends upon it.

The Jesuits from whom I had fled, in disobedience, were good to me. For their Master's sake they gave me a last chance, and I will tell about it.

After my flight they waited a while, a few weeks as well as I can remember, to give me time to think over what I had done. In those few weeks, were I other than blind with pride, I should have realized the folly of what I was doing and the pain and harm I was causing to others.

Apart from high spiritual considerations, I should have been influenced by the instinct of honor that had been implanted in me as a boy at my old college, Clongowes Wood, in

Ireland. There we had been taught, and I had learned the lesson with the others, that a solemn promise is binding and that it is shameful and dishonorable to break one's pledged word. There, too, I had learned that it is mean and disgraceful to betray.

But blindness and infatuation with the superficial freedom I was enjoying kept me from thinking straight, honest thoughts, and the few weeks given me for reflection were wasted.

The Jesuits were kind.

The Father who was appointed to see me, to offer me my last chance, was an old friend of college days at Louvain. He was one whom I liked and admired and from whom I had received many favors. He was a good man, intelligent, experienced, a little younger than I. Slim, pale, courteous, he had great personal charm and I knew he wished me well.

I was living in rooms in McDougal Street in New York City. He phoned me there and asked me if I would see him the next afternoon. I agreed.

I knew his visit had a purpose behind it. I was a little frightened. Subconsciously, I knew that something very serious was afoot, that time was running out. I thought that my mind was finally made up, that I would never go back; yet I realized that my feet were not set on solid ground.

I made ready for Father X's visit. In my pride, I was glad that my rooms were fairly nice. They were well furnished, clean, and there were a few interesting antiques and bits of art work. I tidied the sitting room and placed cigarettes and a tray with wine and glasses on a table. It would be easier for me, I felt, if I could play down seriousness and if I could reduce Father X's visit to one of mere friendliness. I wanted to make it, as it were, a casual visit.

Looking back now, I see clearly that this idea of mine was a cunning suggestion of the devil. It was diabolically cunning! What could render Father X's task more difficult than an attitude on my part of casual indifference? That kind of barrier between us would be more difficult for him to surmount.

When Father X knocked at my door, I was sitting waiting for him, smoking, and, of course, a little nervous. I let him in, greeting him somewhat shamefacedly. He was kind as always, shook hands, and then sat down. He, too, was nervous and paler than usual. The strain told.

Now, looking back and understanding things better, I have no doubt that he had spent long hours in fervent prayer—prayer for me—prayer that God would give him light to see what to say and how to say it. For him, even more than for me, though it should not have been so, the ordeal was severe. He foresaw a host of consequences that I, in my blindness, could not see.

We began to chat, first of trivial things, then about the grave matter in hand. I cannot, after all these years, recall what he said or what I replied. I remember that in friendliness he smoked a cigarette and sipped a little wine. I remember his even temper and how he would glance into my eyes to see if, perchance, he could read any sign of hope.

I think, though I do not remember distinctly, that his gentle persuasiveness began to influence me a little, because I found that I was telling myself to "hold out."

The infatuation of the freedom I was enjoying still clogged my mind. Father X could not get me to wake up to see things as they really were.

It may be that, during the years which followed that interview, Father X often asked himself whether there was any argument he could have used, but that did occur not to him then, which might have moved me? He may have wondered whether or not he had made some mistake, said something that hurt or "injured" me?

No! There was nothing he said that hurt me or that tended to drive me deeper into bitterness. He was a good and kind emissary; none could have done better than he.

There was a letter in his pocket. He had, at last, to tell me about it. The letter was for me. When it was read by me I would no longer be a member of the Jesuit Order. He told me he would have to give it to me, unless—

Father X had not given way to emotion, and in that he was right. Emotion and "beseechings" would have helped none. However moved he was within, he did not betray it save that his kindness grew more and more patient. Then came the tense moment before he had to hand me the letter. Then, moisture filled his eyes.

He was telling me how easy it would be . . . would I not come back with him—back to Campion House. There I would be welcome again . . . no one would remark on anything . . . Father Y was waiting for me . . . He had a heart of gold . . . he had the power to absolve from my fault of running away . . . Father Y wasn't— couldn't—be hard on anyone . . . Couldn't I— wouldn't I—come?

I have often thought about that last appeal which Father X made. Grace was near me then.

Would it had been nearer! Would it had filled my heart!

It was tragic how Father X handed me the letter. Is it imagination, or do I accurately recall those strangled, jerky movements of his hand—to the button of his coat—to his breast pocket—then tremblingly coming towards me, with the letter in it. Then, very serious, sad, and pale, he went away—and I had the letter. I was no longer a Jesuit. My friend was gone.

That was *my last chance,* and years passed before I saw a Jesuit again. Christ had held out His hand, reaching for me to bring me back. I had stood away from Him and fled.

Now, I was indeed a Stray Shepherd. Were my friends glad—such friends, I mean, as seemed to encourage me to make the break?

The Stray Shepherd finds out sooner or later that the mistake he makes does not bring good or joy to anyone. His seeming friends regard him, though they do not tell him so, as an embarrassment. There is an aspect of sheer egotism in his flight that is more calculated to disgust than to please. Besides, he is more than likely to be a very morose companion and a not inconsiderable nuisance to his new associates.

2

FACING LIFE

THE PRIEST WHO BREAKS WITH HIS SUPERIORS and quits his duty is faced at once with the problem of making a living. He has foreseen the seriousness and difficulty of that task, but has said to himself: "I will make my way among men, on an equal footing with them. If others can make their way in the world, I can, too!"

Priests in the world, however, are hardly on an equal footing with other men. They have no professional training for worth-while business jobs. They are not engineers, accountants, technicians, and they have no references to show for previous worldly employment. They are totally without experience in the art of finding a satisfactory position. Their skills are limited and not readily marketable. Their learning is mostly in the fields of theology, classics, and history. They seldom are endowed with such outstanding literary ability that they can easily step into journalism or story-writing.

Priests who, as priests, published books and articles, find that it is one thing to satisfy a Catholic publisher or editor and quite another thing to create the stuff that non-religious publishers or editors want. When they submit manuscripts, they receive them back with discouraging comments. The clerical style and mode of thought is heavy, stilted, confined. No training is less suitable for the writing of "popular" stories than that of a priest. His learning, his logic, his tendency to explain and teach, all render him inept for light literature.

In his eagerness to become self-supporting, the Stray Shepherd is likely to experience ill luck. However shrewd he may consider himself, he is outsmarted by men with a deep know-how in business. He is an easy prey for cheats.

Soon after leaving, I had the satisfaction of having the manuscript of a book on psychology that I had hastily put together accepted by a fairly prominent publisher. I took this unusual success as a proof of my ability to make my way. I watched with interest the business-like expediteness with which my book was printed and issued. My triumph, however, was short-lived. The publisher was bankrupt! I never received a cent from him, though he did, as a gesture, send me a few dozen copies of my book.

As another example of how easily Stray Shepherds are cheated, one of my friends, who had a small capital available, purchased a tobacco store in a large city. He was very "shrewd" and careful. He watched the business done in the store and employed experts to go over the accounts to appraise its value. When he was finally satisfied that everything was as it appeared, he bought the store. Within a few weeks, he discovered that he had been swindled. Those with whom he did business were "shrewder" than he.

The Stray Shepherd, failing to make his way as a writer, and finding he is not qualified to teach, tries his hand as a salesman. He hopes to succeed in selling bonds or washing machines. Here, again, he fails. It is not energy he lacks, but experience of the know-how and the know-where. Others can do it; he can't.

Then his lucky day comes; through an

employment agency he gets a position in an office. The job looks good and promises economic security. He takes his place at a desk and faces his work. Now, he tells himself, if he does his work well and minds his business, he will have peace at last.

But, will he have peace? The others in the office look him over. Some of the sharper ones look him over a second time. They seem to notice something a little peculiar about him. Casually, they ask him about where he has worked before.

The Stray Shepherd, however cool he be, is a little disturbed by the notice that is taken of him and the questions that are asked. He wonders if they guess? Some of the office hands have Irish names. They must be Catholics. He'll have to keep out of their way! He examines himself closely—his clothes, his manner, his "deportment"—to see if by any chance he is revealing himself as a former priest. His suspiciousness increases day by day. He decides to wear gayer clothes and to grow a mustache to make himself look as unclerical as possible.

What he sets before himself is all but impossible. In vain, he tries completely to obliterate his "priestliness." The effect on his character of those fifteen or twenty years that he passed since he crossed the threshold of his seminary until the last Holy Mass that he offered cannot be wholly wiped out. Much less can the great part those thousands of memories occupy in his subconscious and conscious mind be so disregarded that he can speak and think and act like other men. Within his soul, there has been an experience so tragic as to surpass all other human tragedies—the experience of flying from God—and that experience cannot but leave traces. He thought when he ventured into the world that he would be just a man, like other men and on the same footing, but his thought was a lie. He is different. He is marked. And others come to notice it.

When I was working in my office as a psychoanalyst, a client often would interrupt the course of the therapy to exclaim: "You look and speak so like a Catholic priest!" Those who said it were not always Catholics; Protestants and Jews noticed "something queer" about my manner. For many years after I had left the Jesuit Order, I was still taken for a priest in disguise by people who knew nothing about my past. How true, even in respect of externals, is the old saying: "Once a priest, always a priest."

The Stray Shepherd in a big office is never at peace. He knows that in the end he will be

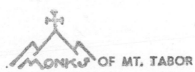
MONKS OF MT. TABOR

recognized and that the whisper will spread around: "So-and-so was a Catholic priest!" After that, he quits.

But he must find money! He has to live! He seeks here and there in desperation. As a last resort, he knows he can pick up some kind of a meagre living if he applies to certain organizations. They will invite him to lecture—to tell his story. He hates to turn in that direction. He despises such "hand-outs." He knows it is a blind alley. I have known Stray Shepherds who preferred to face starvation rather than propagandize against the Church in which they were reared.

Stray Shepherds who take the dole from the hands of the Church's enemies—from those who hate Rome and the Pope with a hate that is at once fanatical and ludicrous—are subjected to humiliation. They are fussed over, of course, and patted on the back, but they are not respected or trusted. They shrink from being called "ex-priests," but, in spite of their dislike to such terms, they are publicized as such. They are subtly egged on to make "revelations" and are afterwards praised for their restraint and fairness in depicting such "revelations" as they know of. Promises are made them, but the fulfillment of these promises is held over. Sometimes, they are defrauded of their retainers.

I remember being invited on one occasion by a prominent New York pastor—I forget what sect he belonged to—to deliver a lecture that I called "The Faults of My Church." I was careful, before I consented to lecture for him, to inquire what the fee would be. He told me that there would be a special collection for me after my lecture. That seemed right and fair, but I was a little suspicious. As a precaution, I brought along with me a good friend, a Stray Shepherd, to watch over, as far as he could, my financial interests.

My lecture seemed to me to go over very well. (How strange it is now to use that word "well.") The chapel was crowded, and faces beamed over my "proddings" of Rome.

When I resumed my seat, the pastor took the platform and, to my consternation, began to tell the most bare-faced (and, for me, humiliating) lies I ever heard. He told his audience how he had known me to be without a bite to eat, in poverty and rags. He told them how he had seen me down-and-out, a broken, hunted fugitive. I can't remember now, of course, his exact words, but the general tenor was as I have written. Then he called upon the audience for a generous collection for his poor friend, the lecturer.

I was on the point of rising to tell the

audience that their pastor's story was a tissue of lies, but something held me back. Largely, it was fear of losing the collection; partly, it was because I didn't want to create a scene. The collector started to make his rounds. I watched. I saw plenty of bills being thrown in the plate and I heard the jingle of silver. But I saw something else. Close on the heels of the collector followed the pastor. As soon as a bill was thrown on the plate, he grabbed it. I looked where my friend stood. He, too, was watching the proceedings, but apparently was unable to do anything in my interest. When the collection was over, there was not a single bill on the plate.

I looked at the pastor and asked where all the bills were. He glared at me in contempt. "Why," he said, "what do you expect? Don't you know the chapel has to be repaired?" The collector, a quiet old fellow who had seen and heard everything, shook his head and smiled. He had probably seen other Stray Shepherds dealt with in that manner before!

The Stray Shepherd, more than other men, is sensitive to indignities and rebuffs. The hard blows of life wound him terribly. He has less resilience than others. Ill luck seems to dog his path. There are so few ways of earning a decent livelihood open to him that every new disappointment is in his eyes a colossal tragedy.

Can it be wondered that some fall by the way, sinking to the depths of despair?

If, in this chapter, the Catholic laity realize the sufferings and hardships that attend the road the Stray Shepherd follows, they should not gloat over the fact. Insofar as they are glad that the Stray Shepherd suffers distress, insofar they show themselves to be unlike Christ. Christ taught us to love and help *all* who suffer. Christ loved the poor. Can we doubt that His tender heart is full of care for His wounded Stray Shepherd? Can we doubt what He wants us to think and feel and do?

Do you know, dear Sister, as you read this in your convent, in the quiet of the evening, that there are priests who are so poor and homeless that they will have to spend the coming night in a flop house, amid the most wretched outcasts? There, on a filthy cot, in a crowded dormitory, amid offensive noises and odors, lies Father Z who once may have absolved you from your sins and placed the Sacred Host on your lips.

Try to see him as he tosses, sleepless on his cot—his worn-out clothes, his ill-cut, untidy hair, his unshaven face, his bloodshot eyes. He is friendless—as far as he knows. He has no money, no prospects. When he groans, as well he may, someone on a nearby cot curses him for

17

the noise he makes. The superintendent, making his rounds under the dim lights, glances at him and sees in him just another bum.

But he is not "just another bum"; he is God's anointed one, a priest!

Now, giving rein to thought, to thought led into a dream of charity, let us watch still a little while. The superintendent has made his rounds, and all is quiet again—quiet, that is, save for varied mingled noises of suffering men. But another figure appears, a grey, hooded figure. We know the garb of St. Francis and his pale, kind face. He is hurrying along, searching for Father Z's cot. Now he sees him, and his face is aglow. Watch St. Francis now! He is on his knees by the cot. He is lifting Father Z's hand to his lips. Now his arms are around the poor priest's shoulders and he is soothing his brow.

Then, St. Francis rises and hastens away to find a bowl of water and a towel. He is quickly back, and busy removing the outcast priest's broken shoes and soiled socks. As he washes the blistered feet, his tears flow. He kisses those feet that wandered from Christ.

Is St. Francis, do you think, smugly pleased that misfortune has followed the path of this Stray Shepherd? Does he nod his head wisely, whispering, "I told you so!" as he looks down on this broken brother? Do you imagine that it was

St. Francis who advised the boss who gave Father Z his last job that he acted wrongly, and that he should throw Father Z out on the street to starve?

Let us finish our dream. Let us listen to St. Francis' prayer as he kneels again beside the cot. "Beloved Master!" he is saying, "Good and tender-hearted Shepherd! Here is one who loved You much while he guarded Your sheep. Now he is in trouble, but still dear to You. I love him and honor him because he is Yours. Take him back in my place and leave me here to suffer his loneliness and sorrow for him."

3

THE BIG GAP

THERE IS A BIG GAP, WIDE AND DEEP, THAT separates us. On one side of the gap are Stray Shepherds, and there are many of them; we are on the other side.

They look on us, for the most part, with resentment and fear. They watch us with suspicion. The gap grows wider as the years pass, and it should not be so. We grieve all the time, and we grieve more and more as we grow in God's love, that they, our dear Stray Shepherds, do not cross over and join us. "What's the matter with them?" we say. "Why don't they come home?"

A few thoughtful Catholics add another, a third, question in such soliloquy. "Can it be in any way our fault that they do not come?"

Some priest reading this, whose brother Tom is a Stray Shepherd, some nun, whose brother Jack left his Order, some old man, whose son Pat fled from his parish, will utter a prayer that I may throw some light on this matter and show in what way the widening of the gap between us and our priests in trouble is our fault. God grant that I may be able to do so!

To begin, let us ask ourselves what is in the Stray Shepherd's mind, or, to put it very plainly: "What's the matter with him that he doesn't come home?"

One of the deepest and most lasting sorrows of the Stray Shepherd is the thought that those who once knew and loved him have turned against him. That is a blighting thought. It poisons his mind. It embitters his outlook. It fills him with suspicion and fear and resentment.

Take it from me, that thought is there. It can't but be.

The Stray Sheperd looks back—in one way or another he is always "looking back"—and he sees the old times when he was assured of respect and kindly affection from those among whom he lived. His relatives—above all, his parents—were proud of him and of what he was doing. The children in his parish looked up to him with trust; they had a smile for him when he met them on the sidewalks. The old men called a respectful "How d'ye do, Father" and the old women murmured a blessing as he went by. He was welcomed when he visited in his parish; he was loved by the pious for his sermons, for his goodness in the confessional, for his gentle exhortations and encouragement.

In those days he had many, many friends among the laity; among the young clergy, he had pals and buddies of college days; among the older clergy he had those who wished him well and with whom he liked to smoke a good cigar and "chew the rag."

That great vista of smiling, friendly faces is now, as he sees it in his morose imagination, changed into a vista of dislikes and scowls and contemptuous sneers. Save in that little corner of the vista where are gathered his parents and relatives, there is no understanding glance. And, alas! even in the faces of his own folk shame and sorrow are seen.

"They don't like me any more," he mourns.

"They regard me as a turncoat, a failure, a disgrace. They distrust me now, and they wish me no good!"

With the years, the immediate agony of this thought of being hated diminishes, but in its stead there grows an obsessional conviction: that every good Catholic is a mortal enemy. The Stray Shepherd becomes a victim of suspicions; he is haunted by something akin to a persecution mania.

Though I, as a Stray Shepherd, still retained a few good Catholic friends, I was so suspicious and distrustful of Catholics in general that I was constantly on the watch lest they should rob or assault me! I remember renting a large safe deposit box in which I kept manuscripts I had written, lest Catholics should break into my rooms and steal them. Whenever I saw a young man loitering near my rooms at night (who, perhaps, was harmlessly awaiting his lady love), I grew instantly suspicious that he was there to do me bodily harm. When Catholics attended my lectures, even those that dealt only with psychology, I told myself that they were there to spy.

Of course, there were things that happened to me—they may, perhaps, happen to every Stray Shepherd—that gave a shadow of plausibility to my obsession that all or nearly all

Catholics, lay as well as clerical, hated me. In these cases there was some imprudence, some lack of thoughtfulness, on the part of those who hurt me, but I had no right to ground a reaction of distrust of Catholics in general on a few isolated instances.

Let me give examples—they may help to instruct such as need a little enlightenment.

It happened in New York City, several years after I had fled from my Order, that another Stray Shepherd asked me to meet a religious on his behalf, to arrange a matter of business. He did not himself want to meet this religious. He preferred that the matter be settled through a third party.

When the young priest came to my office, I received him with real respect. On his part, he was nervous and uncomfortable. He was a very good religious and very zealous, but I could see at once that he was suspicious of me. The interview did not go very well. He became a little angry, suggesting that I was standing between him and the Stray Shepherd whose business I was conducting, although that was not the case. At the time, I would have been delighted to see this Stray Shepherd return to his Order.

Then came the sequel. The priest talked, and what he said was reported back to me. He said openly, so at least it was reported, that while he was in my office he felt that there was a devil in the room. That hurt and shocked me very much.

In that very room I had tried more than once to persuade Catholics who had lapsed into indifference to snap back again into the faithful practice of their religion. In that very room, I had striven as tactfully as I could to steady and comfort priests who were showing signs of restlessness and discontent.

Sometimes, very dreadful letters were written to me by Catholics, letters that were totally lacking in courtesy, while they lacked little in the way of misguided charity. Those letters wounded and embittered me. Worst of all, they widened the big gap that separated me from home.

I think it is the duty of every Catholic to disprove the false idea in the mind of the Stray Shepherd that he is hated and to prove by word and thought and deed that it is not so.

When we show the Stray Shepherd that he is not hated or disliked, but that his memory is cherished and that hearts beat in sympathy and love for him, the width of the "big gap" will be lessened and he will be so much nearer home.

As we have to keep our hearts pure, so we should keep our thoughts clear, lest we misunderstand what is our duty and what is right.

Always, we must distinguish between the sinner and the sin. Assuming, and we are always assuming in this matter, that the Stray Shepherd is a sinner, we should separate him in our minds from his sin. We hate the wrong, the betrayal, the false teaching, the scandal, the disobedience, but we do not hate Tom or Jack or Pat!

Tom (as we supposed above) is a faithful priest's brother. Does this brother not love him still? Does this brother not love him more than ever, and pray for him day and night? Jack's sister is a nun. Does she not love him? Does she not love him more dearly than ever? Is not her heart worn out with its beating prayers to Christ "for darling Jack?" Pat's father is a good Catholic who kneels at Mass every Sunday, perhaps every morning. Has he forgotten his son? Has he disowned him in his heart? Are there no tears in his eyes when he thinks how lonely and lost his boy is?

And those cousins and friends and school companions of Tom and Jack and Pat that knew and loved him long ago—have they really turned against him? Of course not! True, they are sorry for what he has done, but they haven't forgotten him or torn up the pictures they had of him. Generally, they think he will be back home again soon. They conjure up thoughts of what they'll say then, how they'll welcome him.

27

Tom and Jack and Pat would do well to reconsider their idea that the priests, young and old, whom they knew and liked, have turned against them. Priests are not of that nature. They, at least, "make allowances"; they understand. The priest, and I mean nearly every priest, has a soft, pitying spot in his heart for his brother in trouble. He may not be as generous as he feels he ought to be, but he isn't hard and he doesn't hate.

All in all, it is courtesy and affection that we must show to the Stray Shepherd, whoever and wherever he be!

I recall how one night, at the conclusion of a lecture I gave in New York City, an attendant brought me word that there were two young ladies waiting at the door to see me. I asked him to send them up to where I was, near the platform, busy trying to answer a lot of post-lecture questioners.

As the two ladies approached, I glanced at them. I had a vague impression of having known them. They were both very well dressed, and waited together, a little apart, until I was finished with the questioners. Then they came over, smiling. They shook hands with me saying: "Father, don't you remember us? We were in Galway College when you were at St. Ignatius."

Then I recalled them, two prominent girl students of the college, about whom I had had news. They were both married and settled in New York.

They had heard about me, and, seeing an announcement of my lecture, they had come to meet me as an old friend. They were good Catholics. I was no longer dressed as they had known me before, but as a layman. And there was nothing in my lecture that suggested the kind of teaching that a priest should teach.

The past was dear to them and its bright memories of Galway. The present could not have been happy or lovely in their Catholic eyes. But they had learned well their religion and their Christian charity on the old sod. They were gracious to me. They had not turned against me, nor did they hate. On the contrary, all was respect and kindly affection. They knew their part and played it well!

Those two Galway girls threw a good shovelful to fill the gap that separated me, a Stray Shepherd, from my own!

4

OUR HERITAGE

It happens to most of us, I think, that at some time or other we find some little thing among our possessions that we cannot account for. Where did it come from? How did it get there? We do not know. But there it is in our garden or attic or among our clothes, and we like it and are glad to have it.

The little thing that I found of late is like a volunteer flower, a simple pretty flower growing in my garden, come to visit, and, I hope, to stay. It is not in my outside garden that I discovered it with its lovable bloom of white and purple, but in my inner garden—my soul. I have a name for it, and I mean to guard it with care. I call it *Amor Petri*.

Since Peter was kind and good to me, and forgave me and befriended me, I have come to know him so much better. I search out his parts of the Gospel. He is my star there, after Mary, among the human actors. No one showed faith and love as he did. Everything he says and does, from one dark present day to another, is mine to study with dear attention. He is my leader, Christ-given! For twenty-odd years I was alone on a bleak shore—his boat stood off shore—and I never called to him. When at long last I hailed him, he came at once to where I was and took me, kindly and lovingly, aboard his boat. Can you wonder that I listen now when he speaks?

Peter is wise and strong, and he is all heart. He is so much wiser and kinder than we are. He is our Father, and guards our heritage. He tells us about our heritage and shows it to us by word and example. Our heritage is charity.

A short while ago, a Catholic writer, a good Catholic at that, sent me a poem she had written about the cruel treament of Cardinal Minds-zenty at the hands of Communists. In her poem she voiced a reaction that many would think noble, calling on God to avenge the wrong done to the Cardinal and to sweep away his enemies.

But, on the same day that this poem reached me, there appeared in the press words from Peter, in whose mind was the same picture of wrongdoing. What reaction was there in his kind old heart? Did he call down God's vengeance? No! Peter sought salvation for the Cardinal's foes and bade us pray through the intercession of Mary "that those who rashly dare to trample upon the liberty of the Church and the rights of human conscience may at length understand . . . "

No one knew better than I that Peter does not call on God to "sweep away" his enemies. Had I not acted more rashly than the Hungarian Communists? Had I not attempted, by writings, to undermine papal prestige in this country? Was that not a more rash thing than what the Communists attempted when they tried to undermine Cardinal Mindszenty's authority in Hungary?

Peter does not pray for the destruction of Stray Shepherds. On the contrary, he prays humbly like others for their homecoming. His eyes, sunken and strained from long watching, light up with joy when at last they appear.

Our heritage is charity, the privilege and

duty of helping others. It is a priceless heritage, a strange, beautiful heritage. It can never be exhausted. The more that is expended, the more there remains. There is plenty there for everyone, and, if your own are to come first, let us spend lavishly on Stray Shepherds!

Our heritage, then, is to pray for and love and help in every good way we can our priests in trouble.

The first and greatest means of helping Stray Shepherds is through prayer. That we all know, but let Peter, our Father and Leader, remind us of it in his most recent words: "Is there anything that prayer cannot accomplish. What cannot the confident prayer of an innocent or repentant soul obtain when it is said in the name of Christ and is accompanied with good works?"

Since I shall be appealing, directly and indirectly for prayers, endless, earnest prayers, for Stray Shepherds many times in this little book, I shall go on now to suggest, as far as I can, other means of help, so that our prayers may be prayers "with good works" as Peter says.

I think the simplest and sincerest way to answer the question at issue—How can we help our Stray Shepherds?—is to tell from my own experience the things that helped me, meaning, of course, the things that tended to shape my course towards home. They were things spread over the years, but they had an accumulative effect. Mine was no sudden conversion, but, as far as I can see it, the outcome of many influences—the greatest of all of these influences being the graces won for me by prayer.

One of the things that helped me—and I put it in the forefront—was the fact that goodhearted people, clergy and laity, were kind from the beginning, and continued to be kind, to my folks at home.

Need I explain how intensely concerned a "runaway" priest is about the way in which his folks will be treated as soon as his flight is known? Will his people be treated coldly, boycotted, belittled? Or will they be treated "as if nothing had happened," with erstwhile good will and love? He knows that his conduct will not be condoned, but he hopes against hope that people will not "take it out" on his dear ones and make them suffer.

Happily for me, everyone was nice towards my dear ones at home and they acted as if nothing untoward had occurred. I was particularly fortunate, for not a few friendly messages were sent me through my mother. A few "newsy" letters, touching on nothing personal, reached me from old friends. Messages came from others, suggesting that I should visit their relatives who happened to be staying in New York. When Christmas came, there were some cards and simple presents. But, most touching of all, in those grim early days, were letters from home telling of the visits of understanding priests; notable among them, my old Novice Master, who, for all his austerity and humility, stayed to drink a cup of tea with my mother.

A Stray Shepherd is very sensitive to courtesy like that, and his heart and mind feed on it. Sometimes, such things hold tears.

I would place next, among the things that helped me, the friendship, long continued and sincere, of a very exceptional Catholic. He was a successful business man, middle-aged, scholarly, and with a very charming personality. He was a daily communicant, a man of deep faith and piety. He knew all about me: how I had left the Jesuits, how I was excommunicated, how I had written things that were disloyal and bitter. But, nothing seemed to change his Christlike kindness. He never ventured to criticize or counsel me. He just stood by me, a silent, affectionate reminder of better things. Becoming ill, he sent for me. He had not slept for weeks. He wondered if I could help him by my skill in psychology. If I couldn't help, he said, no one could. With me near him, he slept for a few hours.

I missed A.N. very much. Only now do I realize how much he prayed for me, and how much he helped me.

Was he imprudent to associate with a Stray Shepherd? Did he do wrong? For myself, I cannot but think that A.N. did it all for Christ!

Would to God that every Stray Shepherd had such friends as he was! Speaking of friends—but briefly this time—there was another who became a good friend through letters. He lived in Canada, a stout-hearted old scholar of eighty. He came to me through "my door," growling (in his letters) about domineering bishops and some vague scandal he had been witness to. After a year or so, when our friendship was solidly established, he began to show solicitude about my spiritual well-being. Was I praying? Going to Mass? Did I ever think of looking about for "an easy way" of being reconciled? I was surprised at this line he was taking, of course, but I wasn't offended. All he said was in good part. It was well meant. He had influenced my mind quite a little before he admitted who he was, and what he had been. He himself had been a Stray Shepherd! He was, long since, reconciled to the Church, and was now grimly intent on getting me to follow his example. We remained friends until his death.

I think it is a great pity and a great mistake that there should be a custom among Catholics to leave to himself and keep away from a Stray Shepherd. Is it not clear that he will take note of the fact that he is being ostracized? Will that not intensify his bitterness and "widen the gap" between him and home?

On occasion, a Catholic friend would get in touch with me and ask me to come to an Irish meeting, but it did not often happen. It was good for me when such a thing occurred, but for the most part I was left alone. There were a few intelligent and strong-minded Catholics who continued for long periods to take my direction in their psychological problems. Their confidence in me did me good. They dealt fairly with me, being satisfied that my guidance was good. On the other hand, several Catholic clients, as soon as they learned about my past, quit me at once, as though any contact with me were evil.

As I see things now, I submit that a good lay Catholic, if he knows a Stray Shepherd as a friend, should be willing and anxious to lessen his loneliness, should ask him at times to a ball game or a show, and, if the Stray Shepherd has some skill that the lay Catholic is looking for, should be glad to avail himself of it. If our purpose is "to bridge the gap" between our priests in trouble and ourselves, surely we should take such steps.

Sometimes a Catholic reviewer has an opportunity of showing more charity than that contained in harshness and severity, when he discusses the writings of a Stray Shepherd. No doubt, it did me good when some of my writings received unfavorable and sarcastic reviews at the hands of non-Catholics; when for instance, H. L. Mencken referred to some of my work as "poppycock." That was a discipline and it humbled me. On one occasion, the late Heywood Broun, years before he threw himself at Peter's feet, snubbed me in public. That, too, was healthy for my soul. On the other hand. when Catholics, apart from criticizing what I had written, indulged in personalities and uncalled-for sarcasms, that embittered and hurt. Such Catholics as wrote those abusive things lost opportunities of helping a Stray Shepherd.

Once I had a word of encouragement from a great and honest priest, a monsignor stationed in Brooklyn. I treasured what he wrote me and it awakened good feeling in my heart. He had often shown himself a critic, a severe critic, but this time he found something good in what I wrote and impetuously he scribbled me a note to tell me so. He didn't say much, just that "he had hope for me now." There was a break, however thin, in the clouds after that.

Surely, my readers will by this time understand the message that I am trying this way and that to convey?

The Stray Shepherd is desperately in need of something that we can give him. He wants that thing; he hungers for it. He had it once, but it is gone. He misses it sorely. His life has not, and cannot have, much comfort without it. He may in his inner loneliness—his humiliation—feel that he does not deserve it, but he yearns for it all the same.

What he yearns for and wants and badly needs is our friendly affection, and at least a little trust. If we can give him so much (and why can we not?) he will be on the road to happiness again.

I have recorded these few instances (and there were many, many others) of things that helped me. But, in this matter, there were misses as well as hits. It did me no good to receive pious books anonymously. Somehow, I felt that the sending of those gifts was an interference and I resented it. Once, a brawny Catholic veteran, whom I hardly knew, more or less forced his way into my office to interrogate me on how far I was observing the laws of my Church. No doubt he meant well, but that did me more harm than good. It, too, was a miss.

How can we ever forget that the heritage of our faith is *Christlike* charity?

5

ENTANGLEMENTS

SOMETIMES, AS WE WAIT FOR OUR TURN OUTSIDE
the confessional, we are suddenly conscious of a
terrible feeling of shame. How can we ever confess our sins? What will the priest think of us?
"He will be surprised and shocked," the devil
whispers. "He will despise you! He will be hard
on you and ask you a lot of questions! You will
conceal something in your confusion and make
a bad confession! Better not to go! Slip out
now! Another time it will be easier!"

Of course, if you were to ask a good friend (or your Guardian Angel) what to do in such a case, he would say to you (with an encouraging smile): "Don't be silly! The priest has heard all these sins many a time! He's not going to be surprised or shocked or hard on you! He is human himself, and will think well of you for doing your duty! Anyhow, it is to Christ you are really confessing, and He loves you!"

Be that as it may, we sometimes continue to wish that we could make our confession in a distant place to a saintly priest, a wise, kind, gentle old priest who knew the world well, and the meaning of human frailty. To some, such a privilege is given! It is given among others to the Stray Shepherd when the hour strikes for him to return to God.

It is to Peter himself that the Stray Shepherd confesses—to Peter in far-off Rome!

Who is there, with a spark of faith, but would confess his sins in humble confidence to Peter?— Peter, who has the wisdom of ages; Peter, who learned his gentleness and kindness from Christ Himself; Peter, who before Magdalen was heard of had made a public confession, "Depart from me, Oh Lord, for I am a sinful man!"

The Stray Shepherd—and like enough he may have a sad and weary tale to tell—wants above all as his confessor one "who knows all and can do all," a Supreme Shepherd to whom he can say: *"Tu qui cuncta scis et vales!"* Enmeshed and entangled as he well may be in a hundred violations of law—human, canonical, and divine—the Stray Shepherd yearns for an absolution that is authoritative, complete, and final, so that hereafter he need never have any more worry on the score of his confession. He wants to be told with decisiveness and finality what he has to do, so that, when he does that, full peace of mind will be his!

During those long two-thousand years that have passed since Christ placed the keys in Peter's hands, Stray Shepherds have traveled to Rome, in person or by letter, from every land and with every kind of story. Many have been bewildering. But, no less unimaginable has been Peter's exhaustive experience; no less incredible, his quenchless love and pity. Nothing is new to Peter, no knot too difficult to untie.

It is the goodness and kindness of the old Fisherman that will appeal most to the Stray Shepherd as Peter pronounces the words of absolution and imposes the all too merciful penance. "Son!" Peter will say, "If I did not love you, I would be unworthy of the Master! If I laid a burden on your shoulders that was too distressing to bear, I wouldn't be acting towards you as the Master dealt with me. Do no more and no less than what I am telling you to do! Now, you are Christ's once more! Go in peace!"

It is not the Stray Shepherd alone who needs faith in the power and wisdom of Peter. The Catholic layman needs it equally. Over and above that faith in Peter he needs humility. It is not for him to feel or, worse still, express surprise or disappointment over what Peter decides. If Peter does no more than call back the Stray Shepherd into his boat, telling him to be content with cleaning the nets, that is enough and that is final. Peter may not again pass the tiller into the Stray Shepherd's hands or bid him steer the boat. He may or may not send him back to the altar, the pulpit, and the confessional. That is for Peter to decide, and let no one question his decision. Peter knows what he is doing, and he knows what it is right to do. Meanwhile, the lay Catholic who has living faith in Peter will not wonder over Peter's decision, but will rejoice that Christ has His Stray Shepherd back home again.

Stray Shepherds would not in so many instances become involved in bewildering entanglements, were it not for the fact that, immediately following their flight from duty, the rebound from their ecclesiastical state to their new worldly life is sudden and upsetting. Many are carried off their feet by the gale of new experiences that strikes them. In confusion and excitement, they act on impulse. They grasp at anything that they think will hold. Eddies in the whirling air make them dizzy.

They no longer see straight. They cannot look on life steadily or see it whole. The old landmarks whereby they guided themselves are gone. Some rashly align themselves with other churches. Some not only rashly, but with foolish improvidence, contract civil marriages. A few follow perilously close in the footsteps of charlatans and thieves. Some are victims of a shallow infatuation.

In this country, and indeed in most countries, the marriage of a priest when legal conditions are fulfilled is duly recognized as a lawful marriage, and the priest incurs the civil and social obligations of other married men. In the eyes of the Church, however, he is not married. His "attempted marriage" only results in his incurring further censures under Canon Law.

Some priests there are who, though yearning in the depths of their hearts to be reconciled to their Savior, find themselves not only married and with children to support, but also engaged in the pastorate of a non-Catholic sect. Their little ones look up to them with trust and love. They need food and they need protection. And to whom are they to look for that but to their father?

This little book would be of no possible use to Stray Shepherds unless this problem were touched upon, for every Stray Shepherd knows of cases among his brothers such as that which I have just now described.

I can hear the Stray Shepherd, married and the father of children, saying: "It's not about myself I care any longer. Were I free, I would go at once and throw myself at Peter's feet. But, how can I do that now? How can I abandon my little ones and leave them to starve?"

There have been cases, and who has not heard of them, where thoughtless Catholics— nay, worse than thoughtless Catholics—have jeered at and insulted "married" priests.

I knew of an instance in Ireland (in minor detail I am changing the story), where a "married" priest lived in a country village. He was a quiet man, a scholar, giving no offence to anyone and living, as he thought or hoped, incognito. In some way, however, one of the children in the Catholic school found out about him and passed the word around. As happens in such cases, a ringleader came forward and led some of the children to where the Stray

Shepherd was walking along a road, reading a book. Names were called and stones were thrown; then the children ran away.

The ringleader's father was a very sick man. He was bedridden, dying of tuberculosis. He was a plain, thoughtful man, a Catholic, of course, no less devout than many others. When he heard of what his son had done, he struggled out of his sick bed. He was endangering his life, but he did not care about that. He searched for and caught his son. Then he thrashed him as he had never been thrashed before. It was a dying Irishman's way of teaching the lesson of this book.

Is the Stray Shepherd, now married, father of a family and a parson as well, beyond hope? Is his reconciliation with the Church impossible? Is his a problem that Peter has never contemplated and for which he has no remedy? One need but pose such questions to find the answer. There have been harder problems than this and greater difficulties and entanglements for Peter to deal with. But in his hands is the power of Christ, and to that power there is no limit.

Dear Father, married according to civil law though you be and parson though you be presently, will you, as I did yesterday (and providentially at that), open your old Missal at the Lesson (*Ezek.* 34:11-16) of the Mass for Monday in the First Week of Lent? I'll quote here only a few lines. You can read the rest at your leisure. *"Visitabo oves meas et liberabo eas de omnibus locis in quibus dispersae fuerant, in die nubis et caliginis. . ."*

Since I have given the text verbatim, I will translate it freely in my own way, substituting "Stray Shepherds" for *"oves"*: "I will go, myself, to my Stray Shepherds and I will deliver them from all the entanglements into which they fell in dark and cloudy days."

It is not the purpose of this book to make vain guesses at what instructions Peter will give to his Stray Shepherd or at what penance he may impose. Peter considers each case on its own merits, and the only constant factor in his decisions is the wisdom and love that inspires them. All one can say here is that every Stray Shepherd has the right to go to Peter, and is assured of kindness if he goes.

And here, though the matter be delicate, it may be apropos to remind the reader that such a Stray Shepherd as I have been discussing, one who is canonically entangled by the fact of his marriage and parenthood, is in particular a fit object for our prayers. The natural cares and anxieties of his life humble him, and open and soften his heart. Hitherto, perhaps, a selfish man, he may now have become tender-hearted and self-sacrificing. Does he not now consider, with deep anxiety, the spiritual welfare of his little ones? Now, God's grace will find an easier entry into his soul. The first great Peter was himself a married man—he will not refuse his powerful aid if we ask him.

There are entanglements other than those mentioned above which may plague a Stray Shepherd eager and anxious to make his peace with God. He may, for instance, be by birth an alien in this land and liable to arrest by immigration authorities. He may be afraid to undertake anything which would involve publicity. Again, he may have been (or imagine that he has been) a technical accessory in some criminal act. The dread of blackmail may hang over his head. He may be sorely in need of wise legal counsel, even while he makes ready to throw himslf at Peter's feet.

There are various other possibilities. The Stray Shepherd may be in need of a good neurologist, preferably, of course, one of "profound and living faith." He may have become an addict of drugs or drink or of some obsessional phobia.. As much as other Stray Shepherds, if not more, he is entitled to our sympathy and help. He, too, has to make his way to Peter though his road be tortuous. Let us offer our hands to lead him as he goes.

Other Stray Shepherds are happily free from such entanglements, but are still enmeshed by the oldest and subtlest and most difficult of all entanglements—pride.

Their hearts and minds are blinded. With lips tightly pressed together, with eyes closed shut, with a few words, and those coldly uttered, they say: "I will not give in!"

Their pride is now a habit—a sad and meaningless habit—but a habit hard to lay aside. The break would come if they learned, as with God's grace they will again learn, that the prodigal did the right and noble thing when he went back to his father. The break would come if they would again watch prayerfully, as Magdalen wept in public at the feet of Christ.

It is a little humility they need, a little humility sweetened and sanctified by God's grace. Christ's heart was "meek and humble." Why do they wish theirs to be other than His?

Are we to sit down now and wring our hands over the entanglements of Stray Shepherds and the scandal they occasion? Or are we to carry all back to Christ and ask Him to tell us what to think and what to do? Will He not tell us, if we do so, that, if "we love one another," there need be no scandal or futile tears?

When the Stray Shepherd returns to Christ a miracle happens—the incredible mystery of love. Christ alone, of all great leaders, is so exalted, so unbelievably trusting, that He not only pardons and receives back a proved traitor and deserter, but, at Peter's word, He recommissions him and reinstates him in a position of honor as though he were one of His best.

6

A FRIEND'S PART

SOME CATHOLICS ARE DEEPLY MOVED BY THE thought of the loneliness of Stray Shepherds. They feel the urge to help them and they cannot resist it. I know one such.

He's a cheerful man, rosy-cheeked, of robust build, with the kindest eyes I've ever seen. He's aging a bit now, in his sixties for sure, and no longer strong. His 'ticker,' as he calls it, hurts a lot—strange, that so good a heart, one so brimful of generosity, should cause pain to *anyone.*

I met him long years ago after one of my lectures in New York City. He came, I suppose by chance, to the lecture. But, once his keen eyes fell on me, he studied me. For a time he wondered about me. Then—his hunches are remarkable—he guessed my secret. He waited, after the lecture, until all but a few of the audience had left, and came up to me. He took my hand warmly in his. There was a ten-dollar bill in my hand when his was gone, but he was still with me chatting profusely and genially.

He came again, to another lecture, waited to see me, and enquired where I was living. When he called to see me, he carried with him a good, old-fashioned, home-made cake and a bottle of wine. He made me promise to visit his mother and himself, in Long Island.

His mother, a dear little lady, was frail and delicate. She had not long to live. He surrounded her with loving care and did all the heavy work of the household. Pretty, indeed, was the feast we three had together, and when it was over my friend showed me his garden. It was a small garden, but there were a thousand colors in it. There was a dainty fish pond, too, and, of course. a bird bath.

In his study there were several shelves of erudite books; well-thumbed they were, for my friend read carefully and seemed to remember all he read. He knew too much for me about everything. Bewildering he was in his learning.

He soon came to know my Stray Shepherd friends in the city. He cultivated these new acquaintances and managed to do a few good turns for each of them. Strangely, however, none of us knew precisely where he stood in the matter of religion. He seemed to be a Catholic of a very broad pattern, but, for all we knew, he might have been an agnostic with an interest in mysticism.

In time, my friend and I saw less of one another. He remained in Long Island for a little longer, while I drifted away to California. But we never wholly lost contact. At intervals, letters from him reached me, always interesting, learned, quizzical, and, invariably, almost illegible. The constant factor in all these letters was the loving spirit in which they were written.

When my long exile was over, and the Church mercifully received me back, my friend was one of the first to write to me to tell of his great pleasure over my happiness. But he wrote in such a way as to leave me still in doubt as to how far he and I now saw eye to eye in religious matters.

This uncertainty about my friend's religious

status tried my patience. In my new-won enthusiasm I put aside restraint and frankly wrote to him about what was uppermost in my mind. I say it with a sense of embarrassment. I wrote urging him "to return" as I had done. No doubt, he had fun over my letter—or, perhaps, in his humility he felt that it did him good. Anyhow, he kept on inviting more and more outpourings on my part.

At last I "saw through him" and was happy to realize that my friend was one of Christ's very dear friends—one whose obsessing thought was how to bring down to earth more and more divine love, of which, as he likes to say, "there is no measure."

Then the letter reached me that provoked this chapter. Written it was in my friend's usual quizzical way—a little of this and a little of that, a reminiscence or two, and, casually told, a story that stirred me to my depths.

I hadn't read far in the letter when I knew there was something afoot—something had occurred which had made my friend's heart brim over—for he began about one of his hunches "that never led him astray."

But, having thrown out that hint of something coming, he veered off to tell me about his garden—his patch now is in the outskirts of Chicago. Well, his garden "was never so good. . . blooms in abundance. . . .everywhere he turned, color upon color and tall tulips in groups adding height to the display."

Then followed a line about his "always running into Stray Shepherds," and then a sudden switch to Our Lady of Perpetual Succor. He had, he said, to get a good-sized, framed picture, one that looked "ikonish, rich, devotional, Greek, and recalling Athanasius and the defeat of the Arians and the great celebration of the victory, tapers unnumbered, Byzantian chants, and incense and exultations." He added that the Redemptorists were coming to give a Mission in his parish and, "come what may there can't be a Redemptorist Mission without Our Lady of Perpetual Succor."

To get his picture my friend went into a corner of the city where "there is an East European mixed colony, Poles, Slovaks, Hungarians, Lithuanians," in which corner he had noticed a little store where pious objects were sold. The store, when he found it, was very neat and clean and, as he entered, he heard hammer-tapping on metal from a room at the back—evidently a little workshop.

Out of this small back room came the storekeeper, in his shirt sleeves, a quiet unruffled

man of past forty, well-built and fair-com-
plexioned with "a broad, innocent, guileless
face."

"Well, sir, what can I do for you?"

"I'm after a framed picture of the Perpetual
Succor!"

"All I have are on the wall behind you," the
storekeeper answered.

My friend turned to look at three copies hung
on the wall and selected the one that was the
best framed and oldest-looking. The storekeeper
took it off the wall and proceeded to wrap it up.
My friend watched him, noted something
"different" about him, saw or fancied he saw a
trace of sadness, of emptiness in his face, and
felt that he did not belong there. When the
parcel was wrapped up, my friend said gently,
"You are a Lithuanian—Father!"

The storekeeper looked up quickly. There was
a pleased light in his eyes. "How did you know
that?" he asked.

"Perhaps it was from your accent," my friend
murmured, and went on rapidly to tell him of
Lithuanian friends he had and of the beautiful
Lithuanian church in Bridgeport, Connecticut.

"Oh, yes! We have many fine churches," the
storekeeper remarked proudly. "In Penn-
sylvania, too!"

My friend then told him about two bright Lithuanian boys he knew who were being put through college by their uncle, a priest. The storekeeper seemed to approve this, saying "Ye-es" and "describing a circle with his chin."

Soon, the priest, a storekeeper in shirt sleeves, was leaning against his counter, completely won over by this warm-hearted stranger, unburdening himself of his sad life story, and telling of old times in his homeland. He told, too, of dreadful recent times, of his own folk "forced to live like animals," of poverty, persecution, and murder. "I saw it all—I was there," he said.

In slightly foreign accents the story went on and on. "I like my store here," he continued. "The street is bright and busy, and it is difficult to be lonesome. I do a little engraving on medals and rings behind there. It keeps me busy. It was very hard at first, but I do well enough!"

"Would you like to go back?" my friend ventured.

The answer was prompt, and frank. "Sure, I'd like to go back if I was positive of re-admission. But one has to live and, if I'd lose my store, how could I ever make a new start? I'm here ten years!"

Like other Stray Shepherds, his mind suffered

from the old, old phobia, the delusion that the Church was against him and felt ill-will towards him and would be harsh. In this priest's mind, too, the devil had planted that poisonous thought.

"Sure I'd like to go back," he repeated, "but the Bishops are so busy and the examinations are so protracted!" But, as he spoke, there was a wistfulness and a yearning in his voice—the eternal nostalgia of the Stray Shepherd.

My friend's letter continued. "He told me a lot of things. At last, I had to break away. To make him see that I still valued his ordination I did a strange thing. I think I quite dumbfounded him. I asked him for his blessing!"

The priest's eyes moistened. He lowered his head, folded his hands, and recited a long-forgotten formula. Then he made the Sign of the Cross over me. I just grabbed his hand to my lips—the one he blessed me with. I left him then, promising I'd make a special mention of his name the following morning at Holy Communion. Father J. rushed away into the rear room, and I into the street. As I was turning, I caught a glimpse of his little room, the one at the back of the store. I saw a small bench, his work-bench for engraving and a half-made bed.

The room apparently was windowless. I am
so sorry!"

But my friend will go to see Father J. again.
"I will visit him," he wrote me since, "and I'll
bring him an inconsequential gift, a nice fresh
layer-cake, something fleeting, and of course, I
can never gaze on my Lady of Succor without
thinking of him, my poor Stray Shepherd."

7

A MOTHER'S PART

It has come about in Catholic life that a deep bond exists between a mother and her priest-son. This bond is not one of mere natural affection. It is spiritual, as well as human. It is holy and altogether admirable insofar as it reproduces the tie that bound the mother Mary to the great First Priest, her Son, Jesus.

As Mary watched over her Son and brought Him with her to the temple to pray, a Catholic mother cares for her son and teaches him to be good. And there is many a priest who owes his vocation to the piety and inspiration of his mother. As Mary, when Jesus ran away, went in search of Him sorrowing and reproved Him, many a Catholic mother has plucked her son, a priest-to-be, from danger and corrected him. In one great historic case, a mother, Monica, sought her son, sorrowing, for seventeen bitter years. She saved him and in so doing gave to the Church St. Augustine.

Only those "who haven't any brains" (to use St. Ignatius Loyola's quaint comment in this connection) doubt that Mary came first in Jesus' thoughts. And only those who are singularly ignorant of human nature doubt that in the average priest's thoughts his mother likewise comes first. His steps towards the altar from the seminary gates to his ordination are, for his mother, mysteries of joy. His steps up the altar, when at last there arrives the day of his First Mass and the holy words of the canon that he reverently utters, are her mysteries of glory. If his mother's heart is ever to be transfixed, if she, like Mary, is ever to undergo the great mystery of sorrow, it will be when, and only when, he abandons his duty as a priest.

When first she hears the news that her son has fled from his sacred duties and gone into the world as a layman, she cannot believe it.

Surely, she thinks, there is some terrible mistake? She recalls his piety, his faith, the good things she has seen in him and heard about him. Her habitual image of him standing by the Savior with his head resting on the divine breast comes back to her. How can she believe the story she is told?

But, as days and months pass and there is no sign of her son resuming his duties as a priest, fear and torment fill her heart. She weeps and prays. Her one thought is how to save her boy, to bring him back to grace.

"Who is the man who would not weep on seeing Christ's mother in such sorrow?" (*Quis est homo, qui non fleret, Matrem Christi si videret in tanto supplicio?*) What Catholic must but be touched with sorrow when he thinks about the sufferings of a Stray Shepherd's mother? As the years go by, she continues to weep and to pray, and it is hard to think that "the child of those tears" can be lost. From morning to night *he* is never out of her thoughts. All her pious yearnings are about him. Even when she makes the Stations in her church, going from picture to picture, she is watching, as it were feverishly, to see if Christ will carry His cross all the way to the very end and not give in, so that He may save her boy.

Meanwhile, her son writes to her and tells

her "in part" how he is getting on. She writes back, and, if she is wise, she refrains from making reproaches. She wants to tell him that her heart is breaking, but her better judgment warns her against indulging in any form of self-pity. She tells her son to let her know whenever he wants any thing, and she sends him all the news she can think of that would interest him. She would like to write to him every day, but her better judgment warns her against overdoing it.

On his side, the Stray Shepherd knows that his mother is hurt and suffering, and he is deeply grieved to have caused her pain. He is not a cruel monster, a black-hearted wretch, a clerical Caligula. He is human; he, too, weeps; he strikes his breast; he prays. But he has made a false step, wildly, rashly, and now he feels himself trapped. He would, as it were, "do anything" to save his mother from sorrow and shame, but he can't see a way out—and he doesn't want "to go back."

I know there are mothers of Stray Shepherds reading these pages with beating hearts, searching every line to discover some hint as to how to save their priest-son, now, before it is too late. I can even hear their questions poured out to me. Should I send him books—you know the kind I mean? Should I get a very holy priest I know, who is going to the place where my son is, to visit him? Should I myself go to see him? Should I throw myself on my knees and beg him to come back? Should I pretend to be very ill and send for him to come to see me before I die? Will you write to him? Maybe he would listen to you?

To most of these questions the answer is "No." A Stray Shepherd wants to be left alone. I "hated to be interfered with" (I looked upon it in that way) by literature or arranged visits. Meetings that happened by pure chance or through Providence were different.

The part of a mother in saving her priest-son is to pray and to be kind and loving and patient. Once in a long while, she might send a little pious picture. Near me now, as I write, I have such a one that my mother sent me, but I just hid it away in a book. If it ever should happen that the priest-son in a letter opened the way for a word of advice, the mother would be wise to ask her boy "to drop into a chapel once in a while to hear Mass."

My mother died after twelve years of *apparently* fruitless prayer for me. I know the spot where she is buried. It is a little family vault that I visited a few times as a boy. It lies in an old Catholic cemetery, a wooded place, between the Dublin mountains and the sea. It's near a village, and children passing by bow and cross themselves, murmuring "May they rest in peace!"

The vault towards which my thoughts so often turn is far away and no road leads to it for me. Likely it is that I shall never be able to kneel there to say as I would say with great loneliness: "Mother, dear, I'm sorry."

It's hard to think now of all she had to bear in the way of pain and disappointment during her last twelve years. The golden years for her were the years when I was a priest active in my duties and she thought those golden years would last for always. But, the worst of blows fell and her head was bowed in shame. She was always gentle, hating to cause any harm or hurt to others, but it was she who was chosen for this cross. I think she bore it as bravely and cheerfully and sanely as any woman could, but that doesn't mean that it didn't break her heart.

About ten years after leaving my priestly duty, I went to visit her in Dublin and spent whole days together with her. She had aged, of course, and her voice had not the gay confidant ring of the old times, but she was still bright and full of "go." She had never a word of reproach for me and never openly cast a disapproving glance at my lay attire. We drove to the mountains and to sea-side resorts, and dined together in pretty places. We went into shops to buy little presents, and together we knelt to pray at Our Lady's shrine in Clarendon Street. It was like old times, only that she tired too quickly and suffered too much when it got cold.

One day when we were driving through a lonely part of County Tyrone we ran into an electric storm. There were frequent flashes and the thunder followed close on the lightning. I noticed that my mother had her beads in her hands. Her face was calm and serene as she prayed. Then came a blinding flash. A bolt had struck near where we were.

"Are you frightened, mother?" I asked.

She looked at me and smiled in her gentle way. "No, son! I'm not afraid when you are with me!"

At the moment I felt the love and trustfulness of her remark: it was not till later that I realized its deep meaning. Then I saw that she had told me, as only a mother could, that in her eyes I was always God's priest and that she had faith in me. Maybe in that moment, when death was so close to both of us, she was given the grace to foresee that in God's good time He would deign to recall me to His service.

My mother's words—"I'm not afraid when

you are with me!"--sank deeper and deeper into my heart. They gave me hope and courage. They taught me, too, the lesson that I am trying to convey in this chapter, that a Catholic mother has great, perhaps almost irresistible, power to save her "Stray Shepherd" son.

Like other Stray Shepherds, I knew that my mother did not and could not look upon me as hopelessly wicked and *lost*. I knew that *in her eyes* my sin was not one of real malice, but rather of disobedience and wilful folly. Like other Stray Shepherds, I knew that my mother loved me dearly, that she was "on my side" as far as in conscience she could be, and that she wanted my true happiness and good above all things.

What wonder if in return I trusted her more than I trusted any other human? What wonder if the feeling I found in my heart towards my mother is likewise the experience of many another Stray Shepherd?

Twelve years is a long spell for even the most patient and brave of martyrs. Her heart could stand so much, and no more. It was not of any well-defined sickness that she died. The doctor who attended her was puzzled. All he saw was that my mother was losing a battle. There was nothing he could do. When she received her last Holy Communion, her eyes were filled with joy and love. She told my brother that she was very happy. That was the last thing he heard her say. Her death was sad news to me, recognizing as I did that she had died when her poor heart was worn out with playing gallantly her harrowing part as mother of a Stray Shepherd.

8

THE WORKING OF
GRACE

WHEN I CONTRAST THE TWO PERIODS OF MY
years in exile—the decade that followed my
flight from duty, and the decade that preceded
my petition to Rome for pardon—I find a
striking difference.

In the first period, swayed by pride and bitter
with resentment, I shed my religious practices
one after another, till little was left. I found
excuses for this and that omission. With callous
insincerity, I pretended that it was impossible

for me to say the Office. Neither morning prayers nor night prayers were remembered. Trivial pretexts sufficed to excuse me from Friday abstinence or hearing Mass on Sunday. While I never denied the faith, I soon began to make little of its bulwarks and defenses.

My trouble, in essence, was not that of losing the faith, but rather of neglecting and abusing it in my struggle for such money and fame as I could win. I was reckless about the harm I was doing. I trusted vaguely that my intentions were good and that people would not be misled or scandalized by anything I said or wrote. Like many another Stray Shepherd, I doped myself with the narcotic of sophism.

Turning, now, to the second period, the decade preceding my homecoming, I find that there arose in my heart, uncertainly at first, then very surely though slowly, the urge to pray, the nostalgic need to worship God. The prayers and sacrifices that were being offered for my conversion were taking effect. There awoke a gnawing hunger in my soul.

A Stray Shepherd such as I was, lonely at heart and bereft of confidence, finding himself drawn towards God, naturally turns back to the oldest and simplest prayers—prayers of pure worship and petition. He is conscious of his unworthiness and helplessness. He feels he cannot promise anything with sincerity. He cannot promise to reform his ways or to do penance. He can ask God to look down on him with pity and to forgive, but he dares not undertake to love God in return. He cannot make the Act of Contrition though he can strike his breast and cry *"Miserere mei, Domine!"* Also, and this is his greatest comfort, he can say the *Pater Noster* from beginning to end.

The *Pater Noster,* our greatest prayer, is the sinner's prayer. Christ knew that when He made it! When I found that the *Pater Noster* fulfilled my need and that I could say it all, every word, with sincerity, I used it with ever growing frequency and fervor.

It was but a step to the discovery that the *Ave Maria,* the little sister of the Lord's Prayer, could also be said with sincerity. Like other Stray Shepherds, in my state and stage, I did not want to "compromise" myself by making any kind of a promise even to myself of returning to the Church or anything of that kind; nonetheless, I had to pray. It was a great joy for me to be able to say the *Pater Noster* and the *Ave Maria*—and every word respectful, fervent, and sincere!

Then I began to feel that prayer was not enough. Months and years were going by, and a need, even deeper than the need to pray, awoke. To God, to the Father of All, sacrifice, oblation is due. In my soul it once again became clear as day that man, be he sinner or saint, should offer sacrifice to the Almighty, that he should join in the act of supreme worship and homage.

I had never wholly given up going to Mass. Once in a while I would slip into a crowded church, staying on a back bench close to the door. I used to feel frightened and awkward. The fear of illness used to assail me. Perhaps I should be stricken and have to stagger out of the church with all eyes staring strangely at me. In spite of this curious phobia, I would hear Mass once in a while.

Then came the time (God reward those fine, kind people and nuns who prayed for me) when I began to attend Mass regularly, so as to offer up to God the supreme worship of sacrifice that was His due. I offered up the Holy Sacrifice with increasing faith and fervor. Sometimes, even though I still haunted the last benches, I could forget myself and rejoice that God was being fittingly worshipped and honored. Here at last, and here alone, was a sacrifice worthy of God, the old and ever new magnificence of Calvary.

And here, once again, and especially for the sake of my brother Stray Shepherds, I would like to point out that I did not feel that I was "compromising" myself by hearing Mass. My mind was still vague and uncertain about the future. I had no definite plan of seeking reconciliation with Rome. On the whole, in those days, it seemed to me an impossibility. By hearing Mass I was satisfying a real need of worshipping God, but I was not making any insincere promise. I had only to look back on my life to see a graveyard of broken promises. I could not and would not as yet make another. That is the sense of what I said with the words, "I did not feel that I was 'compromising' myself by hearing Mass."

The old Irish proverb says truly that "there is no gain like that of hearing Mass" (*Ni luach go h-Aiffrionn De eisteach*). My gain indeed was great. An old Jesuit in Dublin, when he heard from my brother that I used to go to Mass regularly, smiled. "Then he's all right!" he said. The Mass means so much in every way, in his heart and mind, to the Stray Shepherd that for him to hear Mass is a fast step homewards. Were it possible that the mother of a young priest in trouble, who had quit his duty, could exact one little promise from him before he fled, the promise she should ask him to make, I think, would be just this. "Promise me, Son, that sometimes you will slip into the Church, in disguise though you may be, and hear Mass!"

It was fortunate for me that my home during this period of my exile was located in a typical American Catholic parish. The Catholic population was not large, but it was devout. There were few Irish in the parish, but, in the number of Sunday Communions which I watched carefully, it was well on a par with, if not better than, the parishes of the old land. It came home to me that the faith was strong here, as strong as in Ireland. It came home to me, too, that American priests and nuns were doing splendid work.

Like many another from Ireland, I brought with me a curious snobbery about Irish Catholicism. In my eyes, Irish Catholicism was the real thing, unique and above anything to be found anywhere else. There could be, I was convinced, no such Catholics anywhere as in Ireland.

Now I began to see that I had no right, never had any right, to assume such spiritual superiority in my own people. Had I not in my own personal history a lesson to reflect upon? Around me, here in America, I had evidences of magnificent faith and virtue, thriving amid every possible allurement of materialism. Without disparaging in any way Ireland's marvellous fidelity to her grand heritage, I began to see that snobbery over that fidelity could and should be replaced by sentiments of deep humility.

Step by step, as I regained the habit of prayer, my thoughts and sentiments changed back to those that belonged to me in sober years. Mentally, I now adopted the Catholic viewpoint, "the Church's side," in national and world affairs. Often, I was furious over the blatantly unfair criticisms of Catholic action that appeared in the press. Anything that seemed to hurt the Church hurt me. I vowed that I would never again write one word "against the Church," and I kept that vow. An offer came from a publisher to issue a condensation of one of my books in England. I refused. I was now beginning to take control of my destiny and to take an independent stand toward those whose favor I once cherished. Old loyalties were rekindling; now there was a fair flickering of hope.

At this time, by way of added graces, there

were several occurrences that may seem remote and trivial to the reader, but that were important and significant to me.

There was the occasion when I called upon the pastor of my parish for the first time, to request him to offer a Mass for the repose of my mother's soul. He knew about me, and when I entered seemed not a little surprised. He made me sit down and began to ask me how I was getting on, and so forth. He seemed afraid to let me say a word. He insisted on asking if he could be of any help. Did I need a little financial assistance? He put his hand into his pocket searching for his pocketbook. His charity was running away with him!

When I could get in a word, I explained what I wanted, and he was very relieved. He would have been pained to think that I was in trouble. He chatted in the friendliest way and, when I was leaving, told me to drop in any time to see him.

The interview made me feel good. My pastor had treated me as a human being, one he could talk to freely. He even seemed to trust me!

My first words to a Jesuit in twenty years were spoken in a real-estate office. The realtor, a Catholic, introduced us. The priest, a tall, handsome man of middle age, was, I believe, from Alma College in California. He shook hands and chatted with me in a very friendly way. He was cordial, without overdoing it. He said he had seen me about—which meant that he knew who I was. I was no ogre to him, no villain, no would-be dagger-man. I might have been a member of a club he frequented, a friend whom he was glad to meet again. I was deeply affected by this little interview with a Jesuit and felt good over it. I had the feeling that God's saints were sympathetic and well-meaning towards me.

If he had refused to meet me, if he had rejected my outstretched hand, a dark despairing wail would have arisen in my heart. But he was not like that. He was kind as Christ was when He said to the woman of Samaria: "Give Me to drink!"

Once in a while, I received letters from American boys whom I had taught at Georgetown University in Washington, D. C. I did not always remember them very well—too many years had passed. But they remembered me and cherished kindly thoughts. They knew, of course, the tragedy that had happened since those far-off college days, but they made no allusions to it. I was still an old "master" to them and it was tactful respect they showed towards me, as well as affection. Fine Catholic gentlemen they were—may God reward them! Their letters did me good.

Then occurred an experience that I now look upon as a very great grace. How unexpectedly, and strangely to human eyes, does God's grace work!

I had been chopping wood on my Californian ranch one September afternoon. I had worked too long and too hard in a hot sun. Weakness overcame me. I struggled indoors. The weakness increased, and my heart seemed to grow faint. Stimulants didn't help. I was numb, and life appeared to be ebbing. It seemed to me that the end was at hand. I was going, for sure! My mind turned to God and I struggled to say: "Thy will be done!" To my great joy, I found myself resigned and found I could say with deep sincerity: "Thy will, Thy Holy Will be done!" Then, I felt nearer to God than I had felt for eighteen years.

The strange weakness passed. but the experience left a deep impression. Prayers were being offered for me! Grace was being given to me! Now, surely, I should try to cooperate! Now, I knew that I was not abandoned!

Sometimes at Mass, I used to feel very lonely as I watched the *good* people who approached the altar rail to receive Holy Communion. I used to envy them their privilege and the good consciences that were theirs. I still knelt near the door, ashamed and afraid to go up near the altar. It seemed that I was in the church only on sufferance; that I had no canonical right to be there, that I could be ordered out if the pastor so willed.

How I used to watch the communicants! As the pastor distributed the Sacred Host, I could always hear his prayer that made each communion into a *viaticum*. If only I could once again—just once—receive the Sacred Host, too! That thought began to possess my mind. It returned again and again—always insistent, compelling attention. No Stray Shepherd can for long watch the altar rail thronged with communicants without being deeply moved. "There is nothing in the whole world like this," he thinks—and perchance he murmurs:

> *Tu nos pasce, nos tuere,*
> *Tu nos bona fac videre,*
> *In terra viventium.*

The Holy Eucharist is the argument that triumphs.

Those who mock at the Church and at the conversions that grace effects, pretend that it is always the fear of Hell, remembered or stirred up by violent words, that brings a Catholic sinner back to his religion. And the same people pretend that it is only on his deathbed that an errant priest ever returns. On both counts those cynics are in error.

The fear of Hell, while an excellent motive for repentance, is but one of many good motives that lead to repentance. As far as I know, the commonest motive is renewed faith in and love for Christ in the Blessed Sacrament. For the Stray Shepherd, more than for any others, this motive is paramount, for he in a special way has known Christ's love and enjoyed His trust.

God's grace worked in my soul through one other thought, and that powerfully. It was the thought that burial would come one day, and that to be buried anywhere save in the shadow of the Cross of Christ was a mean and lonely thing. How could I but remember that those I loved most were all, without exception, gathered to rest under the Savior's Cross? How could I hope that in my turn I could rest in peace unless the Cross, the pledge of salvation, stood above my grave?

Some Stray Shepherds, no doubt, are won

back to Christ on their deathbeds. For that, every good Catholic rejoices, with a joy that is great though long overdue. There are other Stray Shepherds who cannot resist the call of Christ, and who hasten home long before the last bell tolls.

9

HOME AGAIN

HE HAS LEARNED TO WEIGH AND MEASURE values the hard way. His tired eyes and ears have learned from the glib colors and voices of life a shrewd art in telling when an answer is true. Now he, the Stray Shepherd of America, my friend and my brother, has questions to ask me. "What does it feel like being back again? How do they treat you? Is it hard to toe the line? Does being at peace make any real difference?"

I, a Stray Shepherd for more than twenty years, could not, even were I to attempt to do so, deceive him. He has seen and knows too much. But I would not do so, even were I able! Knowing how he has suffered, knowing his straits, it would be inhumanly cruel. These questions that he asks me, and to which he is entitled to an answer, I will answer as though from my deathbed.

Now that I am reconciled to the Church and free to approach the altar and receive Holy Communion as often as I wish, my feeling is that of being at home again.

The word *home* connotes being among things and people that are familiar and dear to you and being there by right—not on sufferance. It is very sweet to be home again after a long absence. Everything is doubly dear, and doubly beautiful. Now, one can rest, feeling secure, feeling that one has escaped from evil and danger. The old walls give one protection. Being with one's own reawakens confidence. Life takes on a friendly glow. No more does one need to hide!

As a boy, I did my schooling in a private college far from where I lived. I spent the terms there, sleeping in a bleak dormitory, eating in a big refectory among hundreds of strangers. It was lonely and hard for a little fellow, but, when vacation came around and I was sent home for the holidays, what a recompense was mine!

It was sheer joy to be home again—to sleep once more in a room of one's own— to awake mornings without any sound of harsh bells or fear of lessons and masters. Then I used to dress hurriedly and run downstairs to the kind of breakfast I loved, then off in the free sunshine to play with those I really knew and liked. To be home again was a wonderful joyous awakening!

The feeling I had then, back in the old house with my own family on vacation, is the feeling that is mine today, though the years have taken their toll in many ways. Lightsome and glad I feel; spring-footed, as it were. And, on a night when sleep is tardy, there is no morose gloom in my heart, but only bright hopefulness in the day ahead.

Has my faith suffered from those decades passed in sullen aloofness from religion?

My answer to this question may be hard to believe, but it is true. I find faith easier now, and simpler, and more full of love. I had grown sick and tired of doubt and distrust. Now, faith for me takes on the aspect of the most desirable thing on earth. Faith means a vivid nearness to Christ, to Him Who is full of pity and love for a friend who has been in trouble.

Being home again means more than handshakes and cries of "I'm right glad to see you!" It means, above all, being able to steal into the chapel to kneel as close as may be to the tabernacle. It means having Mary again as your Mother and Protectress. It means having the saints again as your friends.

One reads in books that returned wanderers grow tired of home, after a little while, and long to set out wandering again. If they tire of home, it is because their home remains the same from day to day and never opens up a new vista for them.

But, for the Stray Shepherd who comes home, it is different. The home to which he returns grows lovelier every day. For he is ever rediscovering forgotten treasures or finding new ones. It is as though the bracing air improves his sight and his hearing and gives him a growing zest. Though his hands be stained and his cheeks lined, the door of his heart swings easier than ever on its hinges to admit impulses of charity.

"That's all very nice," a Stray Shepherd says to me at this point, "but how do they treat you? What about the 'sour-faces' and their moralizings?"

I can't answer this question properly without first recording an astonishing discovery I made when my "return" was made public. It should not have been a discovery or a surprise to me. I should have known of it and expected it. Had I not often preached on this very thing? Had I not taught others that the Church is holy? That the Church is Christ on earth?

I had taught that doctrine, however, without understanding it. It was only on my "return" as a prodigal son that I understood the holiness and love that *is* the Church.

My "return" meant, in the average Catholic's eyes, something that gave happiness to the Savior, that made Him glad! And, straightway, the Catholic heart rejoiced! Such is the tender sensitivity of Catholic love for Christ! My "return," the "return" of any lost sheep, was calculated to thrill the heart of every good Catholic. In the hearts of those thousands who had drawn very close to Christ, there was an exuberance of joy. Tears of gladness flowed: hands were raised in praise; heads were bowed in thankful adoration. Everyone could see in my "return" the picture of the Good Shepherd carrying home His sheep. Every Catholic loves to see that picture; few can see it without deep emotion.

Now, I am asked: "How am I treated? And

what do the 'sour-faces' say?" When every Catholic is glad, for Christ's dear sake, are they not likely to be nice to me? Do they not see that Christ's arms are around me? Are they, even the "sour-faces," likely to be disagreeable towards me in such circumstances?

I received letters—many, many of them. Had I been in doubt about the holiness of the Church, my doubt would have been made ridiculous. Those letters suggested to my mind that there was "a milky way" of saints in Catholic America. Many a time it was hard on my eyes reading them. Letters from priests, letters from nuns, letters from busy merchants and professional men, letters from mothers of families and from office girls, letters from college men and professors, letters from soldiers and sailors and airmen—each one who wrote did so because he or she was glad for Christ. To me they were loving letters, letters to a long-lost brother, saying in effect: "Welcome home! We're overjoyed you're back! We'll never let you go away again!"

Letters came from pastors (those supposedly hard men who spend long hours over account books) that revealed them as simple, holy, interior-minded priests. To be welcomed home by good men "of your own cloth" was touching. Letters came from nuns, modestly telling of years of constant prayer and never-failing faith that the Good Shepherd would find His stray sheep. Some nuns told of the sacrifices "other" nuns had undergone, of painful illnesses heroically suffered for the same cause. There was a simple old nun who had kept my name under a statue of Our Lady for two decades and more. Another nun, dying of cancer, had submitted to an operation so as to suffer and pray a little longer. As always, throughout the Church's history, Christ's Sisters in their hidden convent cells go hungry and thirsty for His sake.

Among the letters and their messages of gladness there came many a heart-breaking cry to me for help. "My son was a priest," a mother would write, "and he is gone! Won't *you* help to bring him back?" Even from a convent, a like cry would come. "My brother, a priest, he was so holy. I've offered my life. Won't you pray?" If only I could publish those letters and show the anguish that a Stray Shepherd causes in the hearts of the holiest and the dearest! Surely, by now, he must know that through the Communion of Saints a great dragnet is out for him and many a willing hand is at work.

In some letters the writers took time out to grow reminiscent. One convert told me how his conversion was assured, or practically so, by the warm charity he observed in a priest's remarks about a certain Stray Shepherd whose name my correspondent brought up. Another convert wrote me that he had been in a Protestant seminary and had there found in the library a book by a Stray Shepherd on the Church. The book so awakened his curiosity that he had gone on to study Catholic doctrine —with the inevitable result. Another convert told me how she had been deliberately and in the kindest way guided straight into the Church through the advice first of one and then of another Stray Shepherd. May God reward and bless them for everything good that they do!

I still have to fill out my answer to the question: "Is it hard to toe the line?"

Are there humiliations? In a way, yes, there are humiliations—but they are not always of the kind one anticipates. There was one humiliation I had, but it was so "good-humored" if I may call it so, and so subtle!

I had expected, of course, that one of the conditions of my being received back into the Church would be the public repudiation of all that was scandalous and unorthodox in my writings. I was, of course, and still am, ready and willing to submit to this condition. What happened? Peter did not say a word about my *famous* writings! I imagine he did not think they were important enough to call for a repudiation. I think he smiled good-humoredly, guessing that I'd be a little humbled over the fact that my writings had not been taken very seriously!

There is another "humiliation" that I have to undergo daily, but it is quaint and does not amount to very much. My present parish is a small one, but the chapel has always a little group for early Mass, which my pastor allows me to serve. As I kneel behind him, happy to be serving so near the altar, my thoughts sometimes wander. I wonder what the people in the pews behind us are thinking. They see a little grey man who has the Latin responses pat on his lips and who is smarter at the rubrics of serving than the boys are. Surely, some of them must suspect something. The little man must be a priest who got into trouble; now he isn't allowed to say Mass!

At the altar they see "the good priest," old, but erect and graceful, performing with humility and dignity the highest office that is the lot of man to perform. He has been faithful, all the time, and he it is who takes the Sacred Host in his hands. Good people, as they pray, must think that the little grey man is doing penance for whatever he did. Let's hope they wish him well and pray for him.

Meanwhile, the little man prays for "the good priest," for all the thousands, the hundreds of thousands of "good priests," the loyal, faithful ones that never quit—those brave old-timers who give God every morning the infinite glory of the Mass, who with all their faults (and no one of them is perfect) remain true to Christ!

"What is it like being back again?" I could go on, as it were, forever telling of "rediscoveries."

In some mystical sense, the returned shepherd brings a fresh mind to the wonderful impact of religion. Things he did not notice or relish before carry rich meanings. Suddenly, he sees values in devotions or saints that he had overlooked.

The Church's hymns, the great ones and even the simple ones, are laden with new import. The *"Stabat Mater,"* the *"Lauda Sion,"* the *"Veni Sancte Spiritus"* move him and comfort him. Sometimes, the final refrain of a half-remembered hymn will carry him away. Some long-forgotten association, mysteriously linked with his heart strings, turns him into a poor, sobbing fool. I know, though

I'm not prone to weep, that when driving home from Mass and trying to pray a bit as I drove, a few lines of the old hymn *"Immaculate! Immaculate!"* came back to me and I could hardly control the wheel. Why should we not gladly admit that there is emotion in religion? In everything great in life great emotions are involved!

The Stray Shepherd's experience makes him shrewd about *values* in saints. Instinctively, spontaneously, he turns with deep respect to pay homage to St. Thomas Aquinas, the solid champion of the faith, the tender poet of the Eucharist. There is a saint the Stray Shepherd admires! A humble, kindly man, a brilliant intellect, a human lamp before Christ in the tabernacle. Who put the mystery of mysteries more simply and sweetly than Thomas:

"O! Res mirabilis; manducat Dominum

Pauper, servus et humilis."

One more question that I have to answer remains: "Does 'being at peace' make any real difference?"

Being at peace does not mean that your physical pains, if you have any, are cured, or that you have a better house to live in, or a newer model car, or more money to spend. It doesn't mean better health or more riches. Neither health nor riches of themselves bring real or lasting peace. But I think every Stray Shepherd knows all that as well as I do. Being reconciled to the Church may in some cases entail great sacrifices. Some Stray Shepherds will have to give up the work they are doing in order to secure peace of soul. Peter knows that. He cannot promise gold for gold. He tells us: "Silver and gold I have none," but what he can give he will give and he can give peace of soul.

The Stray Shepherd who sacrifices all for his soul's sake and comes—old, sick and impoverished—to Peter, will move Peter's heart to the depths. What Peter has he will share with him, crust for crust; of that there need be no doubt. Christ more than once told Peter where to find fish, and on occasion took him to where he could find rest. And Christ is still and always will be with Peter.

Meanwhile, "being at peace," having once more a conscience that is clean and enlightened with God's grace, gives one courage to face the hardships of life. No threatening mishap is terrible any more, no disappointment too bitter to bear. So many fears and anxieties and doubts are gone. The air is good now. Life has a true meaning. In Keble's pretty image, "you carry music in your heart!" All that makes a real difference.

I think that truly decent men have a fundamental wish "to do some good" with their lives and a fundamental fear of adding, through the lives they live, to the bad and evil that is in the world. I think that Stray Shepherds—certainly every one that I knew—belong among those "decent men." But, when a Stray Shepherd comes back and lines up again with Christ's soldiers to lend a hand in the great conflict that is going on to defend God's honor, he is no longer in any doubt about his doing good instead of evil. *He knows —he is sure now—that good is coming out of his life.*

Being at peace does make a difference. It gives you back your self-respect, the infinite comfort of knowing that you are trying to do good. Of course, you still know or half-know your failings and liability to sin again. But, along with that knowledge, there is renewed faith in the Good Shepherd and your own deep experience of the fact that He will take care of you.

The tender, the beautiful, the incredible value of being at peace comes home to the Stray Shepherd when he, still in disguise, a

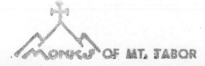

poor unknown, kneels among plain people in a little church, one among thirty at the altar rail, to make his *second* First Communion. Then he will hear Jesus saying to him: "At last! My own friend! At last!"